Off to Dadu's

*Carefree Childhood Memories with
Grandparents, Relatives, and Nature*

By
Balaka B. Ghosal

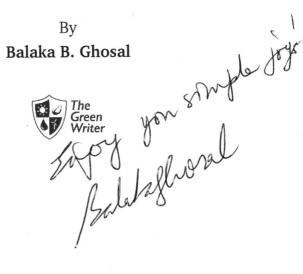

The
Green
Writer

Off to Dadu's

Carefree Childhood Memories with Grandparents, Relatives, and
Nature
First Edition

This is a memoir. The moments described are not ascribed any particular date and time and they merely reflect the emotional interpretation of the author. The names and characters in the book are real but without any historical reference to dates and without any intention to malign or hurt any sentiments.

Cover design and illustrations for the book have been composed by the author herself. A few photographs have been added with permission from family members who were willing to share them here.

ISBN 978-1-7363867-1-2

Library of Congress Control Number: 2021925232

DEDICATION

With love to those special people—
my grandparents, Dadu and Didima —
whose wishes and efforts,
and some deep, intuitive treasures
they hid in their hearts,
made so much of peace
a possibility for all of us.

And to Babua,
our forever-caring, kindly cousin brother
who always added joy without judgement—
and yet had to make a sudden exit
in the pandemic,
without a goodbye.
His life, well spent with our grandparents,
imbued the spirit of giving
with an inimical, never-fading smile
through his short 50 years.

*****

Reviews

1. Off To Dadu's, was a delightful journey of time and space, enticing all the senses and imagination with rich, vivid descriptions of a child's sweetest, fondest memories growing up in India. The culture, family values, reverence for life, all instilled and finding their way into the writer's consciousness of how they shaped her are beautifully interwoven in the telling of this little slice of heaven.

– **Esperanza Smith**, *Holistic Healer & Educator, Executive Director and Founder of PureEsperanza, NFP (pureesperanza.org),Chicago, IL, USA.*

2. It is very relatable as I also had nearly the same kind of childhood visiting grandparents during every summer vacation. The book portrays our culture, our countryside, the food, being submissive yet having the urge to explore, not confined to bookish knowledge, family bonding through music and foodvery detailed writing, explaining every aspect indicating a very happy childhood. The book has a beautiful message that kids of this generation could learn from.

– **Ruma Chakraborty**, *Senior Customer Service Specialist (Retd.), Minneapolis, MN, USA.*

3. Balaka Ghosal shines again, taking us back to our childhood days. At this time and age when families are torn apart by COVID, politics, and internal wrangling, Balaka, in her own free flowing style, takes us back to a world when family meant support, laughter, kindness, caring and sharing. A book for all ages to enjoy and share.

– **Dr. Mousumi De**, *PA-C, MBBS, MPhil, DMSc,*
BSA Hospital, Amarillo, TX, USA.

4. Balaka Ghosal, you have written an extraordinary book! In all the books I've read, I dont think I've ever come across one written entirely in free verseand it fits perfectly with the story! Your memories of visiting your grandparents reminded me of similar trips I'd made to my grandparents when I was young. Your stories are pure joy, especially when you talk about your relatives, young and old. Your descriptions were so detailed I could easily see myself in your scenes even though I've never been to India. I loved your drawings also, done with a wonderful humorous touch. If you miss this book, you'll miss a rare gem.

– **Pam Shannon**, *Natural-Health Copywriter*
and Content Contributor

CONTENTS

ETCHED IN TIME

Looking back into the pages
of my life,
the good old days
of childhood holidays
spent in Kalyani
spring back to life.
With love, I remember the days
spent at my grandparents' suburban home
in the lap of the lush green town.
The colorful memories,
in all hues and shades,
weave a charming quilt
of endless warm moments.

Senses soak up images like a sponge.
For each intense moment,
senses borrow from each other.

It's hard to spot where one perception ends
and the other picks up.

Like the rusty-red scent of the local train.
Or the tickling taste of earth
from the first monsoon rain.
These mixed sensory collages
lend me their magic
to turn moments into memories.

Our little joys and laughter,
along with quiet ponderings,
resided in respect.
In our acceptance of people,
seasons, and things.
And the other realities of life.
Deep intuition seeped into life's daily flow
of humdrum routines and processes.

Life was just as good,
or perhaps way better.
Without the gadgets
and the speed of modern life.
Our imagination tucked in the folds of time,
with hope and wonder.
And a pinch of fear
for the things we didn't understand.
Our silent questions hung around
without the smart answers.

Nature's beauty weaved itself
in our days spent
in the backyard orchards.
She spun us in
with her spontaneous charm.
Her splendor made us happy
with less to own.
Without fancy or waste.

It was an era of childhood contentment—
a spontaneity and openness
I've always wanted to hold on
well into my adult life.

Looking back,
my childhood at my grandparents'
was a time well spent.
The everydayness of their loving care
in those bygone happy times
has helped me be
in my own world of bounty,
enjoying an indefinable richness within me.

Call it a philosophy or a strategy,
this little sneak peek
into those back-in-the-days traditions
lets me understand
my personal green streak

running through life.
Like the threads of wisdom
handed down through the generations
weaving into a beautiful fabric
to wrap these scattered odds and ends
in the labyrinth of my thoughts.

Content and simple,
we had room for calm.
To wrap our seeds of hope through life.
And to help them germinate
as humble offerings of loving service.
My grandparents—Dadu and Didima—
modeling for us in natural spontaneity
the ideals of poise
through life's surprises and fatigue.
It could only be possible
for a reservoir of spiritual strength
somewhere deep within,
a secret they never openly shared or preached.
And yet,
it made itself known in strange ways,
each time we cared to look.

The free verse offered itself
as the narration style for my story.
After years of waiting,
it simply showed up one day,
as if it meant to be.

And I felt an instant resonance
somewhere deep within my soul
with the natural rhythm of the days
the memories hold in the book.
As I wrap my memories into these lines,
I hope it does the same for you,
striking a chord of bonding
with moments of your own life,
somehow, and somewhere deep down.

Balaka
From the heart of Texas.
September 7, 2021

CHAPTER 1

THE TRAIN RIDE

I loved the rusty-red scent of the local train
that took me to my grandparents.
It had a whiff of joy mingled in.
And an instant swing forward.
All the way to my Dadu and Didima's
big, bright home
in Kalyani—a faraway town,
tucked in nature's warm lap.

I was then
a little girl...

We rattled past tiny towns
and peaceful villages.
Tracks lined with farms,
cottages, trees, and ponds.
Ducks quacked and waddled in ponds
next to the frolicking kids.

Their wading ripples crumpled
the reflections of fluffy clouds—
reflections that the algae-green waters
had held still with care.

The dhopas washed piles of clothes
at the ponds' ghat steps,
thrashing the clothes
on a slanting rock face.
Their deft, young wives
spread the six-yard sarees
and nearly-as-long dhotis
out to dry on the lush green meadows.

Their little girls
helped them with the chores
between waving at the passing train.
And hoping to ride one someday.

Cows wandered in pastures
drenched in shades of green.
Crows rode on their backs,
pecking on fleas
that the cows swatted with their tails.

Their boys were busy being busy
with boy things—
frolicking in the ponds, chasing ducks,
playing with frisky goat-kids, or flying kites.
They battled over the prized kites

that glided down, lost and limp.

On the train, the hawkers
either sold savory snacks,
or fruit slices with pink salts,
and large, zesty, spicy brown,
sweet-n-sour, lemony lozenges
that scraped our tongues.
We sucked on the lozenges
till our mouths were bumpy and raw.
Others sold colorful knick-knacks
of all kinds that won our attention.
The vendors hollered in style,
with rhymes and chimes,
while beggars sang their doleful lines
over the rattling wind and
people's endless chatter.

I leaned on the crusty-rusty window rails,
meeting the wind on my face.
The roasted peanuts
our mothers bought
in old newsprint cone-pockets
disappeared in minutes
into our hungry, waiting tummies.

Busy town streets paused
each time a train passed their leveled crossings.
Their traffic bulged on either side
of the clamped railings,

with people watching the train ride high
over honking cars, cycles weaving in between
to get ahead at the crossing gate.

We waved wild
to the eyes that locked with ours,
our minds spinning tales
of dreams that ached with hope
in the nameless lands we left behind.

CHAPTER 2

THE HEART OF KALYANI

An endless chug-n-huff later,
the train ambled, slow and gentle,
into the single-line, tree-laced station
of Kalyani.
All still and quiet around,
the train shushed into her own brief silence.

Kalyani glowed
under the dancing dappled light
of the forest clearing
as we stepped onto
this thin slice of paradise.

Under the giant saal and mahua trees,
that tiny spot on earth
felt like a piece of heaven.
A sweet, earthy aroma
filled me up

with every breath,
my eyes closed,
nostrils flared.

Then came the long, impatient rickshaw ride—

Wheels squeaking and clicking,
with each push of the pedals.
While our hearts raced lickety-split
to where we knew
they were all waiting—
Dadu and Didima,
Chhotomoni and Maima,
Lokkhididi, the house-help.

And the best of all—
little cousin brother Babua
bursting with spirit.
So would be Lalu, the street dog,
and his busy, happy tail.

We jaunted past fields and elegant houses,
restless hearts beating
with every swish from the wheel.
Riding into the hazy horizon,
we went past the Town Hall,
the library, the post office.
And the row of sweet shops,
where we stopped to pick some.
Our necks craned to reach ahead,

beyond our little bodies that stayed
perched on the rickshaw seats
the rest of the way.
Until we circled around the Central Park.
Dadu's home, we knew then,
wasn't far any more.

The rickety rickshaw wheels
whispered longings for love,
softly scraping forward
on the black asphalt,
my tiny heart thumping
with every passing moment.

Soaking into the silence
of the narrow alley,
picturesque houses
stood among the trees
assuring me all was well
since we left last time.
The rickshaw man
ponk-ponked his air-horn
to announce our arrival
just as it screeched to a halt
at the big front gate.

Warm sounds of joy
erupted in the house.
Fondness poured into the front porch
from warm cheeks

and open arms
coming down the steps.

"Chhotomoni," my uncle with many names—
"Mejomamu" for many of my cousins,
"Chhorda" to all his younger siblings,
and "Montu" reserved for his elders,
bellowed his welcome greetings
with shouts of sparkling laughter
rippling through the neighborhood.

I was the only one to call him Chhotomoni.
Chhotomoni, meaning a tiny gem,
has a story behind the naming.
He called me Shona, a nugget of gold,
like everyone else in the household,
but he added a "moni" to mean a gem
and the young-thing me, as a child,
reciprocated the special affection
adding the same "moni"
to what I mostly heard
the grown-ups call him–Chhorda.
It was a game we played
around these crazy names,
our affection taking turns to feel the charm.
And soon, Chhorda-moni, shrunk up
in my lisping tongue to become Chhotomoni,
and that stuck for life.

"Maima," his wife,
our quiet and ever-smiling aunt,
had all her loving emotion
in her eyes, large-n-languid,
like the ponds we'd passed.
Her face beaming into a gentle smile
assured us of ample loving care.

Little Babua,
the youngest of all,
shot through the grown-ups
his zesty holler-n-cheer riding over ours.

Lalu wagged hard
from the side of the road,
prancing around the human huddles,
crooning to our mutterings of love.

Greetings and sweet nothings,
cheek-squeezes, kisses,
and feet-touching reverence of pronaams,
weaved between our
hugs-and-more-hugs.

Nose-tingling spicy aroma
wafted from the kitchen,
our tickling appetites
gurgling in sweet anticipation.

My happy vacation had just begun.

I shot through the whole house,
peeking into every room,
on my way to the backyard orchard,
and into the shadowy arms
of deep imagination.
Where she ruled—
In her backyard kingdom,
all green and wild,
in the busy grove
of mangoes and bels,
grapefruits and jackfruits.

The world of the cities
shut itself far behind.

CHAPTER 3

THE BACKYARD KINGDOM

Our play knew no end in the garden.
It was a wild domain for
our dreams to lift off with the breeze,
sway with the branches
and feel the swings of the seasons.
Fantasy ruled over the dark shadowy kingdom
under the mango, kathal, and bel trees.

Without rules, without fear,
with an abundance of love-loaded carefreeness.

The door that led to the garden
from the pantry
always remained locked from inside.
The three large steps from the garden side
were our own outdoor parlor
to catch our breath

between our play,
and to try out
the first tarty mangos of April.

Sinking our teeth in their tight, sour flesh,
or even raw cranberries and aromatic limes,
we cherished their flavors on our fingers
long after we'd sucked on them.
We chewed on, our eyes squinting,
dabbing in the salt heaped in our left palms,
lips puckered in extreme sour delight
till our teeth squeaked, stinging raw.

We'd dream of the peak summer months,
when the mangoes would get ready to ripen
their sweet, flavored flesh
before the verdant days of monsoon.

The kitchen window facing the backyard
always smelled good.
The steamy starch from the rice pot
flowed down the sink
into the narrow, open storm-drain
skirting the garden,
its hot-rice aroma wafting past our noses
between our fairytale adventures
fanned the ravenous hunger.
We gulped saliva by the mouthful

to pet and calm our appetites.
The symphony of lilting stirrings
of steel ladles, pots, and pans
sounded heavy with nourishment.

While we played on,
The backyard patio got busy.
The outdoor wash area
near the kitchen window
had the buckets lined up.
White sarees with ornate colorful borders,
white punjabis and pajamas,
and the all-white bed linens and curtains too
would be soaking long enough
in soda and boiling hot water,
to be dutifully pounded
to their spotless best.

The sarees hung high
on the lines across the patio
letting us play hide and seek
between their crisp folds.

The same wash area after meal times
took its role as the spread out kitchen sink.
where pots and pans
gleamed and blushed
after a powerful mud-n-ash scrub

from Lokkhididi's powerful hands.

Under the dark shades of trees,
stood the spare bathroom with its tiled roof
and small windows beyond our reach
with no shutters or bars,
inviting birds to make an occasional nest
on its wide ledges
sheltered under the extending tiles.

The large door had a jute-string loop
instead of a bolt
that held on a humongous hook on the inner wall.
An occasional spider in a corner,
it's sprawling web, intricate and undisturbed,
distracted us in the act
of pouring large mugs of cold water over our heads.

It was an ethereal world on its own,
right within the span of the backyard.

CHAPTER 4

YUMMY DELIGHTS

Dadu's home meant food of all types.
Round the clock.
And every single day.
The kalakand squares and kanchagolla balls—
ah, those delightful, chunky desserts
from Bhushon's or Deben's sweet shop,
along with the fried, spicy, flour khasta kochuris
and stuffed radhaballavis.
Didima's hand-made delights—
especially the payesh, pithey, mowa, naru,
and uffra desserts—
were added over the daily feasts.

A vendor came at the doorstep
with his bicycle loaded with tins
full of caramel peanuts

and large rice-crispy mowa balls
that barely fit on my palms.
He came more often
if he knew I was visiting.

Milk came in glass bottles.
They stood in a line, cold and tall,
on the side steps to the stairwell
leading to the roof.
Fresh butter floated
thick at the bottlenecks.

Didima scooped out the globs
with the back of a spoon
and spread them thin
on crispy brown toasts.
My fingers shone bright,
wet with gleaming, melted butter.

At breakfast,
steamy milk from the brick coal-oven
poured thick and creamy
into our steel bowls.
Rich with its orange-hot aroma
of hot coals,
waves of milky vapor
caressed our faces.

We sat snug and tight,
Didima watching every bite
and ordering more from the kitchen,
which "Maima" seemed to magically
supply before our plates were empty.

Family meals buzzed with frenzy.
Krishna mashi, my mom's forever-young sis,
came with her boys, Ani and Shomu,
perched on her bicycle,
their tiny legs dangling
just outside the wheels.
With them came an endless stream of goodies,
and loads of soft cuddles and humor.

At every lunch time,
all the boys had to be rushed for their showers.
No meals until we'd showered and looked clean
was the clear condition.
No wiggle room around that rule.
Our appetites tingling impatient,
we hurried our younger cousin brothers
into competitive two-minute bucket bath challenge,
pouring mugs of water on their heads,
scrubbing their dusty little bodies with soaps
and washing off with more buckets
full of cold water—

the last bucket poured over the head all at once.

The young ones ate first.
Large groups split over two tables—
the smaller hexagonal one
by the window was a favorite.
Didima was always present,
no matter who was eating
and at what time of the day.
She made haste so slowly,
without ever appearing busy,
yet steadily attending to all,
taking care to take care,
while finishing her chores,
and often a whole lot more.

Mothers came in turns with
their pots, ladles, and
generous serving hearts.
Food was always aplenty.

The men ate next,
the womenfolk last—
savoring the unhurried
last scrapes over leisurely chatter.

Even then, there happened to be

a magical supply of just the right amount of rice
and a few delectable items
for anyone who showed up at the door—
a relative's surprise visit
at all kinds of odd hours,
sun up or sun down.

CHAPTER 5

SNEAKING OUT FOR PHUCHKA

We gluttonous cousins,
craved for more spicy adventures.
Sneaking out to Central Park
to seek out a phuchka treat—
our favorite savory,
crispy, semolina balls, empty on the insides
waiting for the fillings,
and then, for our teeth to sink into its crusty depths
stuffed with super spicy potatoes and
dunked in tangy tamarind nectar.

Our young uncle,
none other than Khokonmamu,
being closer to our age,
was the occasional sponsor
of this culinary experience.

A research student then,
with some money to spare
for these ravenous rendezvous
to spoil his crazy-about-phuchka nieces,
and also an occasional nephew in tow.
Sometimes the oily moghlai parathas,
those flat, flaky, flour dough
flipping hot on the iron griddle
were additional surprises
to land on our craving palettes.
We even dunked down spicy, hot rolls
at times—oblivious of their questionable quality.

Gulping gourmands,
devouring a dozen phuchkas or more,
belching and burping,
we wiped our mouths
with the back of our palms,
our lips burning with satiation.
And promising to keep down the story
of this culinary tryst.
Especially working on Babua,
who couldn't ever keep a secret
from the grownups.

Halfway home, Babua's guilt would soar
and win over his prior assurances.
Belly full, and innocent in his reasoning,
"We mushn't lie to our elders,"

he would implore.
Indignant and shocked,
we blamed each other
for bringing him along.
Hesitant to prod him to lie,
as good didis, we older sisters, should never do,
we squirmed in fear
of the elders' rebuke,
petitioning for a plan of deferred honesty,
hoping he'd keep silent
until we'd left for our city homes
on the next day.

No matter how frustrated
and confused we were
of Babua's transparent ways,
in his own inimical, innocent ways
imbued in each and every cell
of his being,
it was quite impossible
to be angry with our sweet cousin.
Our emotions didn't flare,
just a tad bit of chiding.
Though, to tag him along,
we never dared,
on our future outings
for any phuchka affairs.

We were out of luck this time, though.

First, with Babua's announcement
the moment Maima stepped onto the front balcony
to greet us.
Then, our own tummies began to
rumble and churn in a few hours—
our pain betraying our mischiefs.

Our Dadu, a doctor of medicine,
raised his eyebrows,
his tone heavy with shock and fear.
Didima, as his dutiful wife,
and just as aware of germs, in Dadu's association,
chided us for our greed,
and especially for modeling it for little Babua.
Tirades on deadly diseases—
diseases that could rip our guts out—
came from none other than Chhotomoni.

Khokonmamu, the youngest among the adults,
and guilty to boot,
joined them with fake rebukes
to deftly cover his role
as THE accomplice to the crime.
He looked us up, from head to toe,
and jerked his head in disdain,
"How could you, eh?
How could you eat such terrible things?"
While we squirmed at his affectionate treachery,
we knew he'd sponsor another treat

not too far into the future.
Only, and only if we kept it a secret.
Even from Babua.

Maima's affectionate smile behind them all
was the only sweet assurance
we could count on that evening,
vowing never to venture for phuchkas
ever again... which she very well knew
to be a promise we would never keep.

CHAPTER 6

THE PATIENTS CAME

Dadu's home clinic,
was the front balcony.
After his hours at the hospital,
local people came at any time they needed
since his service never officially closed
for the night,
or even in the wee hours of the morning.

Especially for the poor,
whether or not they had any money
to pay a fee.
And he would also go for home visits
to see a sick neighbor, and town folks,
far and near.
Always ready,
even in the middle of his meals.

Tall, black, mahogany, medicine shelves
lined the wall by his bed.
The entire room smelled heavy and somber,
serious about the business of healing.
Back home from the hospital,
on his bicycle or a rickshaw,
Dadu attended to patients as they arrived,
putting aside the scoop of food
he was about to chew,
never hesitating to stop mid-meal
to care for the sick,
to rid them of their immediate agony.

Fear and curiosity mingled
as we watched from behind the curtains,
Didima sterilizing the needles and syringes,
boiling them in water on the kitchen stove,
before Dadu broke open ampules of shots
for the sick who sat huddled in pain.

I heard stories of Dadu's poor patients,
who were unable to pay,
and were keen to give in kind
out of their own, spontaneous volition
to show their gratitude.
They'd bring in fruits from their garden,
or even a bunch of live chickens,
accidentally set free to run around the house,
and a dozen humans in pursuit to catch them,

much to the alarm of our great grandmother
who wouldn't stand them as a devout Hindu widow,
sprinkling the holy waters of the Ganges
to purify the space.

We heard of the days when our great grandmother
helped Dadu with a special medicine
the modern pharmacies couldn't provide—
one that she could make in batches
for burn victims, to soothe and heal their skin,
quite like magic.

It was an ointment made from fresh butter
washed clean a hundred times over
in tender coconut water.
With Didima as her young assistant,
she would spend an entire day
on this complex, elaborate project
all laid out in the backyard,
chopping coconuts and rinsing cold butter globs
to bottle up this brilliant synergy
that soaked up the heat
from the scarred skin,
to beat the germs out,
to reveal the new, baby-pink skin below.
Each time, I'd hear of this Shotodhouto molom,
I'd want to hear the whole process again,
to imagine a line of jars reaching homes far away
with a promise of hope and healing.

We too were Dadu's patients at times—
when lymph nodes swelled up
and swallowing was a struggle,
when the allergies hit hard
or our tummies grumbled.
Dadu peered down our throats,
or pressed around our tender bellies,
ordering the blandest diets
to our dismay and regret.

When one of the toddler cousins magically
chewed and swallowed a full box of crayons,
Dadu had him cleaned out from inside—
had him gulp a good deal of castor oil
the night before—no choice—
to have a pile of crayon-colored purging
under Dadu's carefully supervising eyes.

When Boromama, our oldest uncle,
Dadu and Didima's firstborn, and
a doctor serving the military,
came to visit for a few days,
he'd be the young set of hands to help,
maybe even with a CPR—to save a life,
to bring back a victim of electrocution
from the brink of death
right across the street.
Little did we know how safe we were

with their brain and heart
serving the needs of all around them.

Dadu's large desk had a glass cover
holding many large pictures under it.
Pictures of lands far away—
Saskatchewan, the Sahara, or the Serengeti.

Stories from distant lands
that Dadu wove for us
mesmerized me,
my jaw dropping into the
depths of bottomless imagination.

In the cricket-buzzing silence
of the unhurried evenings,
the monotone drone of the fan
whirring above us,
we gathered around Dadu
to listen to his tales
of his tea garden days
at the railway's hospital
in the Himalayan foothills,
our minds racing back in time,
wandering on the deep, snake-ridden
jungle slopes of the Dooars,
full of stories of the simple folks,
the polite and spotlessly clean bhutia families,
his daring stories of averting snakes

and nerve-racking tales
of treating patients with snake bites.

Bookshelves were all over the house.
In every room. Either built into the walls
or standing tall, lining the walls.
The largest room, the only one upstairs,
that could hold several beds,
study tables, and all of the shelves,
invited the bookworms into endless reading—
especially Chhotomoni
for his own moonlighting passion
for research, and more research,
writing his own book
on unravelling the mystery
of Greek and Latin terms
that enriched the English language.
Terms that are hard,
until they seem easy
when we know what they mean.
He'd often be buried in books
exploring a missing link
in the biological evolution of species,
like the duckbill platypus.
And Khokonmamu too, would spend hours
for his Ph. D in Physics,
researching on a complex topic
we never tried to understand.

Maima and Didima too
caught up with their readings
after all the chores were done
throughout the year, in the quiet hours
which were not frequent.
At least, not for Maima,
especially when we were visiting.
Yet, the local library
would soon fall short,
and Didima would be ready
to repeat her best finds,
advising me to read the top classics
once in every decade of our lives
to find new treasures
with advancing age and maturity.

CHAPTER 7

OUR EVENING SOIREES

Each evening gently came
riding its own chariot of crickets,
their shrill chorus
bidding the day goodbye.
The cool southern breeze
picked up the scents
of nameless wildflowers
from the forlorn fields around.
Men returned from work,
their cycle wheels and
a few occasional rickshaws
scraped a monotone,
in sync with the crickets,
deepening the vibrant silence
of the approaching night.

If a cycle bell tinkled

and the garden gate screeched open
Didima and Dipli, Khokonmamu's mother,
would instantly know who arrived.
How? We never figured.
It was a way of the times
when the pulse of the days,
and the people, were tied
in a certain rhythm that
the folks could feel
deep in their veins.

Evenings meant music time
on the tanpura or harmonium,
and Babua accompanying on the tabla,
his fingers drumming a fine rhythm.
Mother and I, and all the aunts
and cousins of all sizes and ages,
sang their melodious Tagore songs.
Dadu and Didima listened, deeply immersed in love.
Each time we forgot the lines,
and mumbled a fake filler word,
Dadu softly uttered the right ones
surprising us with his limitless knowledge.

Dadu never sang any of the songs he loved.
He often read Tagore's songbook, Gitobitan,
like a book of poetry, his favorite being,
"Ki paini taar hishab milate mono mor nohe raaji"—

like Tagore, he was always ready
to count his blessings,
never ready to list what life denied him.
"Majhe majhe botey chhirechhilo taar,
Tai niye ke ba kore hahakaar,
Shur tobu legechhilo, barebaar,
Mone pore tai aaji."
Yes, life did snap the strings at times,
but why lament for what's missed, it says,
the music picked up the notes, time and again,
it is that vibe the poet chose to remember...
Dadu remained a living legend
of this positive mantra
of sifting life to find only that is good.

The feral cat precisely showed up
at meal times, of course.
She licked her paws by the kitchen door,
fidgeting and bearing her test of patience.
Quiet, smiling Maima, and her silently singing soul
rolled out soft, round, wholewheat rutis
to lightly flip them on the coal fire,
until they puffed up like steaming footballs.
She was ready to feed the hungry cat
and the family on time.
The lizard on the wall stayed busy
on its hunt for the light bugs
and chuckled out loud "tick-tick-tick"

which also meant, "Absolutely right"
in plain, perfect Bengali.

On some rare nights
the phone rang wild.
Phoolmashi, our "flower-aunt"
like we all wanted to call her,
would be calling from faraway England.
Barely older than my mother
by just a couple of years,
she was bursting with energy and humor.
She held her heart in her voice,
her emotions of missing her motherland
across all the oceans,
and all the sweet love of her family
pouring out with every word.
Loud with laughter and also
whimpering tears of joy and separation,
Phoolmashi would wrap us
in a sweet frenzy of emotions.
Her husband, our Phoolmesho,
calm and wise in his demeanor, would join in.
And their three children
with their tenderly-hesitant Bangla,
while I longed to hear the
Blighty accent which was nothing less
than honey to my ears—
something I practiced secretly in the mirror.

Our entire clan assembled for turns
around the large black phone in Dadu's room
that sat on a glass-covered mahogany shelf,
each of us waiting to talk to each one of them,
shushing up all the inevitable side conversations.
We all got a chance
to holler on the mouthpiece,
so loud—we could be heard
in the neighborhood,
perhaps all the way in England too,
even without a phone.

We had so much to share
and the distance so huge,
all we could ask
was the bland "How are you?"
Over and over again.
Sprinkled with "HELLOOO... can you hear me?"
At least a dozen times, for sure.
Our joy overflowing just from hearing
the squeaky, distant voices
on this once-in-a-blue-moon call.

The call was the joy by itself.
Whether we heard them well or not.
And we talked about it for days,
with the same intensity of excitement,

fondness, and fantasy,
thinking of their life in England.
And of their visits in the past.

Family reunions pumped in life
into the quiet days of Kalyani.
Our stories never ended
between cousins our age,
When the football was limp and deflated,
the boys played on, regardless,
with the nearly-ripe jombura,
the big ball-like pomelo fruit,
on the low-hanging branches.
Only to get a gentle reprimand
from Dadu when he found out
his tasty jomburas
were gone after months of caring.
We girls giggled over stories
and planned for pranks
while pickles and cookie jars
emptied in minutes.
Our teeth squeaked sour,
our tummies bent in pain,
we'd admit to the pickle plunder
and promised never to repeat,
forgiven again by our sweet darling Maima,
who always had a vein
to feel our pain

about going by the rules.

On rare evenings,
we would be returning from somewhere
on a rickshaw again,
tracing an asphalt-scraping ride
back to Dadu's big house.
The streets would be sleepy,
the dim porchlights of houses
lighting the way with their pale glow,
and ghostly shadows of trees and lamp posts
sent cold shivers down my spine.
The evening conch-shell blew
from many surrounding homes,
dolefully announcing the close of the day.
Passing by the Buddha park
with its giant banyan tree
lowering hundreds of aerial roots
from high branches
to hold the ground in its place,
I felt assured of a stable and calm earth
that would stay beneath our feet.

On some special evenings,
Didima took us to Shejo Pishima,
my mother's devout aunt, to join other women
for a chant at Shobha Maa's temple.
I'd only stare at the rows of women from behind,

their heads draped with their sarees
as they sang out their lines
I didn't understand. Only watching in awe
the alcoves etched in the walls—
alcoves that held the lamps under their tiny arches
and cast dancing shadows all around.

One night, we went to a play at the Town Hall—
to see a Tagore dance-drama musical.
I was beyond words
recognizing a neighborhood aunt
in the king's robe—
shocked at her complete transformation.
Weaving our way to the greenrooms
behind the stage after the play,
it was strange meeting her in her usual self,
talking and laughing
still in her kingly robe.
It left me mesmerized all the way back,
imagining roles and stories
in faraway fantasy lands.
The night air lent its wings
for my stories to take flight.

CHAPTER 8

SHOWERING MANGOES

Late spring visits were blessed
with tree-loads of raw mangoes
and the raging early summer storms.
In the month of Baisakh,
these kalbaishakhi storms
brought many of the green mangoes down
without any effort.
And the mercury with it,
but only for a day or two.

The storm sent us foraging
for the sour fruits
all over the backyard.
Barefoot and wet,
bucket in one hand and
flashlight on the other,
chattering in delight,

we squealed with every find.
The mangoes were laid out
on the cool pantry shelves.
The house felt rich with the aroma
of the first mangoes of the season.
For days we sank our teeth
in their tough skins, dabbing salt.

Thick, gooey chutneys were added to the daily menu
and the remaining mangoes
were cut in quarters to dry in the sun,
smeared in turmeric to beat the molds.
Soon they filled the pickling boyom-jars
that stood waiting for this event.

The softer fleshy ones were cut in strips.
Thin slices shriveled in the sun until
the turmeric changed to brown
and the salt crystals clung like sand.
These aamshis could be stored in dry jars
for months, even years.
Our mouths watered up
to think of the syrupy sour drinks they'd make
in the non-mango seasons,
to linger the spring memories.

The ones that held on to the branches still
would grow large over the weeks,
turning into soft, sweet orange flesh,

we so loved peeling their skin by hand or
tugging with our teeth while licking
every trickle of their juice
all the way to our dusty elbows.
Like frogs lapping up
an escaping fly.
All before the grownups caught us in the act.

One arm stayed busy
flailing and swatting
the rainbow-colored, jumbo, daddy-sized flies.
With no intention to kill, of course.
They buzzed around, doggedly,
determined to rob their share
of the mango booty.

Summer meant macha trellises
for the long, green, and tender lau squashes.
Their roots sunk in the garden soil,
these squash vines found their way
to the roof top by the water tank,
giving us some cool shade under the trellis
and the fear of a possible lau-doga viper
camouflaged in the look-alike green vines.

Still, there was the lure
to spend lazy afternoons
under its dappled lights
while I held Babua in a trance,

mesmerizing with hair-raising stories
spun in the make belief world
of fairytales and fantasies,
often weaving the plots right then
in a thick cocoon of mystery.

CHAPTER 9

LAZY AFTERNOONS AND LEMURS

A full-belly meal of a delightful menu
sent us into a happy stupor
of long, dreamy afternoons.
Eyes soon shut,
sprawled mystery adventure books
perched on our noses.
Or we snuck out the back door
that never needed to be locked during the day.
Mothers snuggled with their mother, our Didima,
or with their sisters and sisters-in-law,
catching up on their life's events,
finally slouching into their siestas
after a long day at the kitchen.

Bottles of pickles, both sweet and sour,
of mangoes, tamarinds, or green olives,

emptied into our bellies, in the backyard,
and we hung little kittens to our clothes
when we walked over to Chhotodadu-Dipli's
just a few blocks away.
Sometimes even all the way
to Krishnamashi's house
that shared the backwall to Shejo Pishima's,
our Dadu's little sister,
both ready with their pampering affection.

We wouldn't return until our mothers
were stirring from their naps
in the slanting last rays of the day.
It was time for tea for the grown-ups,
and a round of snacks for us kids,
with more tales of the past to share.

Patches of wild berry-groves lay strewn
with ripe topa kools under their tall trees.
I often missed out on these kool-picking outings,
my eyes soaking in a mystery book
lolling on a bed with ornate Burmese teak bedposts
that held faded mirrors to reflect a fuzzy mix
of fear and a burning curiosity of a hidden past.
Or I'd be wildly swaying on a swing
in the tiny Nehru park, nearby,
without a care where the others went.

Until the lemurs came in large groups,

prancing from one garden to another,
sweeping off all the ripe fruits
from the high branches—
of mangoes, jackfruits, and the bananas.
Each time the tall trees shook their heads wild
and rustled their leaves out of the blue,
we knew the lemurs were visiting.

We followed them around,
many yards behind, making faces
and getting a toothy grin in return
that scared us to the pits of our tummies.
We knew very well their grin to be a warning—
a threat so we keep a safe enough distance.

We'd heard of their tight slaps that
left long, neat, blue streaks on the cheeks.
Yet, we couldn't take our eyes off them,
those ash-white, handsome hanumans.
I envied their easy, languid leaping
from tree to tree and the balancing walk
on the thin boundary walls,
dreaming of having lemurs for pets.
Someday...

Mother lemurs, nearly as large as I was,
carried their babies like pendants on their chests,
leaping from tall branches, the babies clinging tight,
their tiny tails swinging.

The big male devoured bananas
while looking over their shoulder for safety,
and tucking two safely in each armpit
as safekeeping—
in case they were chased away in the act,
they'd have a bit to carry over
to their waiting families.
The hard-shell bel fruits, they'd
throw on the ground below
to crack them open,
to get to the yellow, mushy insides.

The way they shared the loot, in precise social ways,
would surely put humans to shame.
The little ones sat in a neat circle around an adult,
their palms cupped together to receive
their little ration in quiet dignity.
As the parent scooped the fruits,
in quick confident strokes, the kids took their bit
while stealing a side glance on their siblings' share,
only to check if their own was fair,
without any tantrum or protest.

Always hungry for more lemur stories,
we kept Dipli, our youngish granny,
talking through our games of cards.
She was our friend, in spite of being
much older in age and by relationship—
Chhotodadu's wife and Khokonmamu's mom.

We prodded her to tell the best of all stories
that we couldn't wait to hear—
of Chhotodadu's tirades
at the police station,
complaining of lemurs
eating up the ripe harvest
of mangoes and jackfruits and
getting snickers in return
from the policemen, who sincerely proclaimed
they were recruited only to catch human miscreants,
NOT lemurs.

Yet, out of respect for the old doctor,
and a dollop of fun, on the side,
they came to inspect, one evening
Chhotodadu's backyard—
the scene of lemur crime.
All piled on a jeep,
they came in a hoard,
to promise and assure that
they'd take care of those lemurs
who had dared to trample
the old doctor's hearty harvest
of the season's best fruits.

All while the family held their bellies
behind the bedroom door,
peeking from the slits along the hinges,

their palms over their mouths
to suppress their laughter and catching a breath.
Chhotodadu, undeterred, felt good,
his heart content to have done his part
in saving his love's labor from future plunders.
We'd mull this over for days on end
recreating every moment in our little heads.

And our hours also rolled
at Krishnamashi's, our youngest aunt,
fondling her many furry, four-legged babies—
mostly Queen and her cuddly puppies.
Our ears picked up mashi's childhood tales
of this town of Kalyani,
of her own adventures in the times
when the lemurs visited more frequently.

We munched and scrunched on
dozens of delicacies, pouring excitement
over some board game,
licking pickles, or spiced up ripe tamarind
with salt, mustard oil, and Chhotodadu's
prized home-grown green chilies that
let out steam through our burning ears.

Losing track of time, we honored the addas,
the freeflowing hang outs, over all other calls
of life's other responsibilities, like
returning home on time.

Until someone came running to fetch us
from Dadu's home, prodding us to return,
adding a caution of a rebuke
for keeping the meal waiting at the tables
with our simply mindless delay.
Most of the time, it was Babua
who came to fetch us, feeling slightly piqued
at having missed out on our fun
to take care of his homework and tests.
As always, he would linger on with us,
totally oblivious of his role
as our fetcher-upper.

The final fetcher would be
one of our mothers, of course,
nearly herding us back to Dadu's,
like rounding up unruly cattle
with an invisible lasso that only
we could feel.
All the way to the waiting tables
and loaded plates of flavorful meals.

Carrom, Ludo, and Chess
occupied the remaining hours in between,
our tournaments running into the nights,
keeping neighbors awake,
perhaps with a tad bit of envy
for all the laughter and falsetto screams
over happy panic and pretend-fury

around our rooftop game sessions.
Even when Didima shushed us up,
we could barely stick to our manners
as we reached the brink of
tensed moments of winning or losing
these friendly boardgame battles.

Before we knew it,
hours had rolled by too fast
until it was time to pack our bags,
pleading in our teary, hoarse voices
to linger a bit longer,
to take the last train out of Kalyani.

CHAPTER 10

MONSOON MIST

The crazy rains came
through the monsoon days.
The first aroma of wet earth
drowned us into a revelry
of memories tinged sweet
in waves of pathos and peace.

We sat in the covered balcony
by the front porch
and sang rain songs
loud and clear
into the howling wind.
Rumbling, spine-chilling thunders,
followed lightnings that cracked
their whip to rip up the darkness,
even if for a second.
We could see the road stretching out in front,

all the way to Nehru Park and beyond,
the rain beating down on asphalt, making puddles.

The strong gust brought them in—
through the wide-open steps
that led to the front garden
along with those misty drops our eyes didn't see.
Droplets that cooled
our skin and clothes—
their moist drape blessing the summer.
The crystal-clear air felt strangely green,
reflecting the leafy hues from all around.

Our rain songs
held a hidden pulse of pain
of unknown people and places
suffering in distant lands.
Especially when the power went out,
plunging us into darkness.
The kerosene lamps with their leaping flames
could barely flicker in the wind,
casting ghostly shadows dancing on the walls.
"Haye pathobashi, haye oti deen, haye grihohara" or
"Khobor eshechhe, ghor bhengechhe, daroon jhorey,
tareri bhashay shonket chhote tokka-tore."
Our hearts heavy with nameless pains,
we heard the wet winds call out to us,
to fly out with them, to embrace the world.

We thronged each time, every few years
when our aunt Phoolmashi
visited from England with her family.
Our joys knew no end, and
affection poured like honey,
blending all the love and laughter
into one perfect smoothie of good times.

All relatives came, every chance we got
in the weeks that followed.
Perhaps even the local train
and the market place felt
this happy tiding for a month.

The dining area stayed busy all day,
and the beds that held three on normal days,
magically stretched to squeeze in five,
and bed rolls took up every open space
in every room, tucked snug tight under
mosquito nets of every size.

I remember cycling out
into the lashing rain,
and three younger cousins for company.
Four crazy cyclists on the lonely
alleys rolled into the main road
equally deserted from the scary,
thundering, pouring clouds.

My wide-border cotton saree
sitting heavy around my ankles
making paddling an ordeal
against the stinging pouring
from the clouds above.

We sang out free on these empty roads,
a few stranded pedestrians as our audience,
huddled under bus-stop sheds,
waiting to reach their homes.

Returning back to Dadu's
to the worried mothers, aunts, and uncles,
we enjoyed being the center of attention
with a mix of rebuke and relief.
A refreshing warm bucket bath later,
and devouring the waiting hot-rice meal,
we told tales of our adventure,
our Dadu enjoying them the most,
encouraging our youthful spirits
beyond the realities of dangers
of all-that-could've-happened.
"If not now, then when?"
was his final assurance,
giving us courage, and
a deep longing to do this again...
someday soon.

Relentless rains found ways to
make Babua more creative
in hiding my mother's slippers,
so she wouldn't be able to leave
by the last train of the day.
Perched on a turned-over bucket,
he'd carefully keep the leathered pair,
snug under an umbrella
in the backyard garden.

Such were the times of love,
twined in the bonds of sweet affection.

CHAPTER II

AUTUMN CELEBRATIONS

The shorter days that followed summer
cooled the mango-ripening mercury
for us to get ready to welcome Maa Durga
on her visit to her earthly home
in the sunny season of early autumn.
The evergreen leaves
were now fewer on the branches.
The shiuli tree by the boundary wall,
filled up with her starry-white flowers
with a peek of orange at the center,
sprinkled dozens at her moist base.

We shook the branches and squirmed with joy,
feeling the graceful shower of flowers and dew.
An intoxicating fragrance wrapped us up
into the festivity of Durga Pujo,
Lokkhi Pujo, Kali Pujo, and Bhai Phonta.

The shiuli garlands we strung and the platefuls of
extra flowers wafted a mystic aroma
in all the rooms through the days, everyday,
all the way from Didima's
prayer room by the pantry,
along with the sugary flavors
of kodma, naru, and uffra offerings.
We snuck up secretly
with the large ollas, those black carpenter ants
that bit hard when disturbed in their quest,
to relish the prasad
from the sweet offerings on the altar.

The tall kaash-grass flowered
in a burst of fleecy-white plumes
announcing the season to the wind.
The sky responded with joy,
painting fluffy white clouds
all over itself.

The marigolds, zinnias, and dahlias,
in their gorgeous colors
thronged the gardens
and the altar,
the marigolds even sprinkled
on the food offering
with the holy basil, tulsi.

New clothes, clean homes,
outings to the community gatherings
in the decorative pandals,
the large dhaaks drums beating in rhythm.
Community meals of yummy, hot Khichudi
offered to Goddess Maa Durga as bhog prasad,
musical evenings and drama nights
charmed the whole week
with warm emotions and zesty anticipation.

The carnival by the lake
on the day of bhashaan,
the holy immersion of the idols,
had its own bustling life—
the buzzing "hajak" lamps,
the phuchkas, again, in some secrecy,
pakoras and kachuris bobbing crisp
on the deep-fry pans on noisy pump-stoves.
All kinds of culinary creations lined up,
their mouth-watering sights and aromas
put our will power to its ultimate test.
The four-spoke Ferris wheel
towered over the fair ground,
challenging the dark sky,
the trees watching in serene disbelief.
Villagers thronged the fair as visitors,
or selling their wares and crafts,
their eyes spinning in excitement.
Loudspeakers blared film songs

and pujo-special numbers,
until we could bear them no more.
Announcements for lost children
or sometimes even parents,
over the hyper chatter of the crowd,
honking cars, busses, and rickshaws,
stunned the dark lake to silence
as it received one beautiful clay idol
after another into its chilly depths,
to return clay to clay in the cycle of nature.

Days of meeting and greeting,
celebrating Bijoya Dashomi,
when Lord Ram clinched His victory
over the demon-king Ravana.
To us little people, what mattered most
were the sweets and savories in every house,
and handfuls of nimki, naru, and shondesh,
even from Didima and Maima.
Going out to meet the neighbors,
and definitely to Krishnamashi,
Shejo Pishima, and Chhotodadu-Dipli,
craving for overflowing food and warmth.
And our ever-joyous Bhanu Dadu,
my mother's uncle and family—
always ready with their simple-n-rich
sharing of free-flowing affection and music.
We sat on their cots, roamed their rooms,
unhindered, without a question.

We peeked into their backyards,
shared stories, laughter, and Bhanu Dadu's
ever-spontaneous songs.

The festive season,
and the cool weather
beckoned us to be out on long outings.
Quite a rare delight to enjoy
a day-trip to the temple of Krishna Rai.
The long bus-ride passing by Bagher Mor,
and wondering if tigers still roamed
to pounce out of the bushes,
to gobble us up in one gulp.
Leaving behind the bustle of Rath Tola market,
we entered the lush green grounds
of Krishna Rai's quiet little temple.
Not so little to my tiny eyes—
its porch, a huge expanse for me to run around
with my arms spread out wide.

By the time we returned,
we little ones were too tired
to keep our heads up on our shoulders.
Even our scrawny legs giving way,
swaying off to slumber, our mothers holding us,
cajoling assurances of the long road ending soon.
Once home, we fell like scraggly lumber,
completely claimed by slumber,
strewn around on beds and sofas.

Our mothers fed rice dumplings
into our sleeping mouths,
with melted ghee and mashed potatoes—
just enough to last the night ahead.

CHAPTER 12

WINTER WARMTH

The chilling cold of Kalyani
was special in every way.
From the hot milk at breakfast
to the quarrelling cats at night
that crept under our beds
next to a window cranked open
by the chilly winter winds.

Thick layers of quilt
wrapped our tight bodies
coiled up in bundles to trap
every bit of warmth in the
creases of our skin.

During the day,
the coal-fired bucket stoves—
the koyla-unoons—infused their
smoky flavors in the breeze,

and a good bit into the foods,
whetting appetites while
stinging our eyes to tears.
Dipli and Maima, always seemed to find
time to knit sweaters and scarves,
caps and socks for the young and old,
for those very dear, far and near,
between their chores this time of year.

It was the season for a burst of colors
in the food, in the garden, in our hearts.
Carrots and beets, cauliflowers and peas
made rainbows on our plates.
Dahlias, chrysanthemums, asters, flox,
mussaendas, periwinkles, and roses
were together a painter's palette in every garden.
Walking past the front patches, our eyes
were glued, our feet barely moving forward.
Especially at Krishnamashi's, where pots
stood in rows, each bloom in its upright best,
under meshomoshai's watchful care,
getting ready for a show at flower beauty pageants.

My city-fatigued soul found limitless fun
in my carefree cycling practices,
weaving through the lanes and avenues,
all neat and straight, in rows and blocks,
so predictable and safe as I paddled on.
More so, as Lalu dutifully ran alongside,

protecting me from the other strays,
to bark at them if they dared to come close.
To say nothing of my occasional adventures—
of ramming into milk bottles
lined up full by a neighbor's gate
in my obsessive careful swerve
to avoid a senior pedestrian.

A quick sunset lulled the nights
into an eerie stupor—a deafening silence
even our singing couldn't break.
Hot meals and zesty stories,
or a joyous reunion around a family wedding,
for Krishnamashi, Kajolmashi, or Khokonmamu.
Endless adda chatting, new clothes,
the wedding shanai wind instrument
played at the venue, charming our spirits,
sending happy shivers down our spine,
stirring dreams in our hearts.
So much of unhindered fun made
our maternal uncles' home, the mamabari,
a happy island of fun and cheer.

Winter meant time for Kashundi—
the hot-n-sour, zesty mustard sauce,
fermenting and waiting
since the peak of summer.
We waited to lick our fingers
when we deftly smooshed the stir-fried spinach

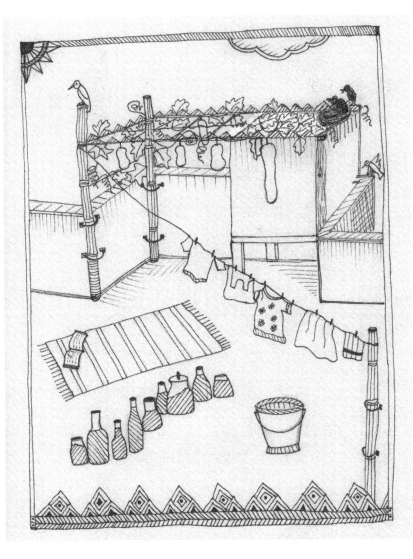

or any other mound of the seasons' saags,
with a dollop of this specialty condiment
only Didima could make
with Dadu's strong-arm stirring
the mustard paste in the big earthen pot—
the pot carefully covered to keep it from rot.
Until the contents were poured halfway
into glass bottles of all girths and sizes,
and left to bake in the afternoon sun
on the roof, all lined up like ducklings,
the bottlecaps loose and tipped to one side
to let the frothing, foaming mustard
find its way up,
pushing out the top scum
like molten yellow lava
flowing down the sides.
What looked seriously yucky,
and even pathetic to taste, at first,
became a mix of bliss, magically changing
our cringing to craving, for more and more.

It was the best season ever for Horir Loot.
The heat and mosquitos staved off for a while,
the whole family gathered outdoors,
sitting on thick, colorful shotoronchi spreads
under the clear, starry sky,
to chant in the backyard by the tulsi-tola,
the perfectly crafted, raised tulsi plant-bed,
offering our love to Hori, the playful Lord Krishna,

with joy and mirth, singing fun kirtans–
"Laaglo Horir looter bahar, loote ne re tora
Chini shondesh phool batasha, monda jora jora!"

As the kirtans picked up the tempo,
we'd be on our edges with expectation
for candies and sweets to be thrown into the air
that we kids would scamper to gather
in absolute frenzy.
We never felt sad if we didn't get as lucky,
in the rush and jostle for the loot,
since we all knew well
Didima always had her pantry full
to make up for the lost loot.

CHAPTER 13

THE THIRTEEN SEASONS OF HAPPY HEARTS

There goes the saying
about the endless ways
of celebrating every day
of each and every month
of each and every year,
for having received something
to be unforgettably thankful for.

So, through the twelve months each year
and the six full seasons in them,
stay tucked the thirteen seasons of fun,
to cherish and relish to the rim
what we receive with love.
Only to give more in return.

Didima, our forever calm grandma,
made sure all needs were met.
From food to the littlest of comforts,
reviewing the checklists for personal care
to their scrupulousest details.
And Maima seemed to naturally blend in that legacy
in seamless harmony of loving and caring.

Our happiness and laughter
needed no power sockets—
they flowed free
with an energy of their own.

Back when our joys
were not stuck in toys,
nor wired to the surge
that now seems to run the world.

The TV hadn't come to stay
on its throne night and day,
holding us subjects,
glued to his court.
The internet too—still in the womb of science,
hadn't stormed in to occupy our lives, and
our fun-fondued fantasies
nestled in the trees and
simmered in the afternoon sun,
warm and fuzzy,

and unhurried moments hung
in the sweet, lazy breeze.

All other cares were met
in profuse abundance
by our elders, rich with their
limitless affection and patience.
They chimed into the harmony
of sharing and caring,
finding joy in every moment
of togetherness.

The rolling valleys
and snow-capped peaks
of the Himalayas,
the lapping waves on the coasts
of our vast peninsula
did call out to us, at times.
But our hearts were happy
right where Dadu called it home.

ACKNOWLEDGMENT

My heartful of thanks
can make a whole book by itself
with plenty of gratitude
on never-ending pages.
To keep it short,
I may have to be forgiven
for not mentioning all
who surely deserve to be.

I'm thankful to all
who made this part of my childhood
a reality for me and many of
my cousins who share these memories.

This little sneak peek into those
back-in-the-days dreamy phase
helped me understand

my personal journey through life.

A thread weaving all the odds and ends
became the beautiful fabric
to wrap my core spiritual journey
with a deep green mission
into a humble hope of service.

I'm indebted to
these priceless moments
that gently shaped me up
to cherish the flow of things
in this whole wide universe.

Though a close resemblance
to my Bengali book,
Chhotobelar Mamabari,
published by Ananda,
way back in 2007,
Off to Dadu's has taken on
a spirit of its own
with many new pictures
showing up alive to relive.

Translating the flavors of Kalyani,
an off-beat suburb of our times,
and to showcase the mix
of typical and innate cultures,

traditions, and sentiments
seemed the hardest of all.
My rough drafts hibernated
for years, without hope.

Until the free verse style
knocked on my creative door
from the pages of the classic—
Out of the Dust.
Although author Karen Hesse
did true justice to the style,
in her depiction of the depressing times
of the Dust Storms during the Great Depression,
I could feel the style in my pulse,
the words nudging the moments come to life.

I haven't been able
to thank her personally.
Yet, this book could be
no less than a tribute
to her and her love's labor.
Without this treasure,
she gave to the world,
I wouldn't dare return
to this sleeping book.
My words began to thaw and flow,
just like the poetic prose
I had dreamed it to be.

I'm thankful for the support
I have from my parents,
my husband, Partha,
and our son, Akash.
Doubly so, because it's never easy
to deal with a writer in the household—
forgetful, without a sense of time,
and always seeming to live in Mars.

To say nothing of the cats,
our Patchupai and Lennybhai,
who lent their unaffected fondness
into whatever I did,
bringing mirth into the mundane.
And finally, of course,
although it should've ideally been
the foremost in line,
I'm thankful to God,
or whatever else you choose to call
the Cosmic Loving Energy,
for giving me a secure childhood,
and the valued family members
who could make these
love-drenched innocent moments
a possibility I could count on.

I don't have words to thank Him—
for walking by my side all along
and making this sweet offering happen.

GLOSSARY

After much deliberation and analysis, and a good bit explained where each of these words have been used, I still felt it would help having a glossary to add some extra information. These words have not been italicized in the book. Current trends in diversity literature is leaning toward blending foreign words in English as a mark of acceptance of new words.

Aamshi—Dehydrated salty strips of raw mango—it was typical to save sour mangoes for the rest of the year.

Adda—Energetic, informal conversation with an intellectual overtone that continues for hours, and is often accompanied by humor and good food.

Bagher Mor—A busy intersection and market place in Kalyani. Bagh, in Bengali language, means tiger. Literally translated, Bagher Mor means Tiger Intersection.

Bhai Phonta—The ceremony performed by sisters for their brothers' welfare and prosperity. Also known as Bhaiya Dooj in northern Indian states.

Bhashaan—Immersion of clay idols that were made for public religious worships. Usually immersion is done in rivers or large lakes.

Bhog prasad—An elaborate, full-course, food offering to God at meal times—usually includes the Khichudi, vegetable curry, fried vegetables, chutney, and desserts, garnished with marigold petals and holy basil (tulsi) leaves.

Bijoya Dashomi—The last day of the Durga Pujo—the day of immersion of the idols—also called Dussehra in north India. In Bengal, it's an important occasion to meet and greet people and visit friends and relatives with sweets and other delicacies.

Boyom—Large glass jar for storing pickles or dry sweet delicacies, like narus and nimkis.

Chhotodadu—Grandfather's younger brother. In this memoir, Chhotodadu was 21 younger than Dadu, and so he held his elder brother in the highest regard.

Chutney—Sweet pickle.

Dadu—The address for grandfather, in general—typically mother's father.

Dhaak—A barrel-sized drum played only during public worship rituals. Two thin sticks are used to hit the drum to create a sharp, high-pitched sound. There's a strong emotional connection of dhaak beats with the joyous feelings around religious festivities.

Dhopa—Washerman.

Didima—Maternal grandmother.

Dipli—A shortened version of a proper name Deepali. As young children, we picked up ways to address our relatives, often without the proper term to address them by. Although Dipli was our grandmother, we called her what her elders called her instead of the proper address—Chhotodida.

Durga Pujo—The week-long celebration around the worship of Goddess Durga.

Ghee—Clarified butter.

Ghat—It's the accessible part of a water body where concrete or stone steps make it safe to step into the water. Washermen have a slanting rock slab next to the steps to scrub the clothes clean—a unique custom to beat out the dirt.

Hajak—A petromax lamp that needs pumping to keep the pressure up—quite noisy, and way brighter, in comparison to the usual kerosene lamps used in households when the power was out.

Horir loot—Outdoor congregational chanting with plenty of finger foods thrown into the air towards the end for devotees to collect. Children, especially, loved the looting frenzy of the event.

Jombura—A fruit similar to grapefruits and pomello. Slightly bitter to taste, even more so if handled roughly. No wonder when boys played football with it, its taste would be too bitter to enjoy.

Kaash—Monkey grass—tall and stately, it grows wild all over Bengal during autumn. Just like the sounds of dhaak beats, kaash is emotionally associated with the autumn festivities.

Kali Pujo—Worship of the form of Goddess Kali, representing shakti or power. It is performed in Bengal on Diwali night, while the rest of India worships the form of Goddess Lakshmi representing wealth and prosperity. The festival is therefore referred to as Kali Pujo in Bengal, instead of Diwali.

Kashundi—A fermented mustard sauce that's very popular in Bengal—mostly eaten with fried leafy greens (saag).

Khichuri—Rice and moong lentils cooked together with vegetables and spices. It has strong healing properties and is customary to offer to the deities during all religious ceremonies in Bengal. Also known as Khichdi in north India.

Kochuri—Deep-fried flat breads stuffed with spices—a delightful snack item for special occasions.

Kodma—White sugar-candy balls. Similar to Christmas red-n-white sugar-candy balls.

Kool—All types of berries. Also see Topa kool below.

Lau—(Pronounced la-oo) Long squashes, also called green gourd.

Lau-doga—(Pronounced la-oo-daw-gaah) Literally, it refers to the curly vines of this creeper. A lau-doga snake, however, is a poisonous one. Its green, slender body mimics the twining vine to camouflage itself.

Lokkhi Pujo—Worship of Goddess Lakshmi, the feminine form representing wealth and prosperity.

Luchi—Deep fried refined flour flat breads.

Macha—A firm trellis-like structure for vines to get a stable support.

Maima—Aunt—mother's brother's wife.

Mashi—Mother's sister—can be both younger or older than the mother.

Mama/mamu—Mother's brother—can be both younger or older than the mother. Mama's wife is Maima.

Meshomoshai—The husband of a mashi.

Mowa—Large, scrunchy balls of puffed rice or flattened rice. These are mixed into hot, stiff, syrupy molasses to make golf-ball or tennis-ball sized spherical delights.

Naru—A special finger-food dessert of Bengal made of coconut and jaggery. Narus can be as tiny as glass marbles or as large as a boiled-egg yolk.

Nimki—Deep-fried white flour squares—very popular savory snack for Bengalis, consumed during social events around the year.

Olla—Common black ants, about one centimeter long, that didn't bite unless provoked.

Payesh—Rice pudding—a special, Bengali delicacy.

Peethé—Sweet-n-soft white flour spring rolls with sugary coconut stuffing.

Prasad—Food received after offering to God. Also see Bhog Prasad.

Ruti—Bengali pronunciation for roti or rolled flat bread made of whole grain wheat.

Shiuli—A native autumn flower of Bengal, emotionally associated with the festivities of the season.

Shotodhouto molom—A naturopathic balm made with milk cream rinsed a hundred times in fresh coconut water especially for burn victims. Also spelled as shata dhauta in English. Molom means balm or ointment.

Shotoronchi—A designed rug, easily folded and carried around.

Tabla—Two-piece percussion instrument commonly played as an accompaniment with music, both vocal and instrumental.

Topa Kool—Round berries in spring, with a slimy soft flesh and a tiny rough, bumpy seed inside—ideal for sweet pickles and syrupy chutneys.

Tulsi-tola—The raised bed of the holy basil or tulsi plant. It's the custom for every household to keep the tulsi plant on its elevated bed and worship it. Each part of the tulsi plant has unique medicinal properties to cure innumerable diseases and is considered to be a divine personality.

Uffra—Less hardened mowa dessert. Puffed rice, called khoi, is loosely wrapped in the molasses' syrup to create this rather unstructured, slightly sticky snack.

A simple translation of the songs mentioned in the book:

1. "Haye pathobashi, haye oti deen, haye griho-hara" – Oh, how unfortunate (this lashing rain) for the street-dwellers, the impoverished, and the homeless. It's a famous song written and sung by the renowned poet, lyricist, writer, and global ambassador, Rabindranath Tagore. Tagore was the first recipient of the Nobel Prize from Asia, in 1913, for his literary work, Gitanjali (Song Offerings).

2. "Khobor eshechhe, ghor bhengechhe, daroon jhorey, tareri bhashay shonket chhote tokka-tore." – The tokka-torey clicketty-clack signals rush on the telegraphic wires bringing news to the migrant worker of his home blown down in the storm.

3. "Laaglo Horir looter bahar, loote ne re tora, chini shondesh phool batasha, monda jora jora!" – It's the time for the loot from the Lord, go for it and get all you can—sugar candies, sweet cheese balls, and pairs of dumplings!

PHOTO GALLERY

One rare picture of myself with my grandparents and Kalyani cousins—Babua on far right and little Ani in the center. Ani's little brother, Shomu, was either waiting to be born or too young. In the early morning hours, Dadu and Didima often sat on these wicker chairs, here, on the garden path that led to the gate.

Two shots of Babua and Ani—always happy to be with each other, even during their shadow-boxing mock-fights.

Dadu and Didima with two of their sons—Chhotomoni on the left and Boromama, an Air-Force doctor, on the right.

[Note: This is not the original picture. In the times of instant digital sharing, I've been lucky to have access to this one. I'm still on the lookout for the original one to replace this. Until then, this placeholder will serve as a reminder of the great souls that made this caring family.]

ABOUT THE AUTHOR

Balaka is a sloth and a chameleon combo. Looks like the spirit of Kalyani has made a home in her heart. And added a twist to her double-helixed fate.

She thrives off of a simple, unhurried, low-waste life poised on her faith of healing from inside, through her storytelling and writing, to share her own passion for reusing resources. Balaka doesn't look forward only to Fridays. Life feels like a blessing no matter how much she gets done every day.

Adjusting to urban life deep in the heart of Texas, in the megalopolis of Houston, Balaka showcases her living on less by reusing resources. She lives close to nature, pondering right in her own backyard, as an extension of her Kalyani days spent with loving human values woven in a peaceful harmony.

ABOUT THE BOOK

Off to Dadu's is a lyrical montage of happy images from the days of simplicity, when life was less cluttered with technology and its over-stimulation with constant entertainment. It's a string of memories from the era when life flowed with the rhythm of nature.

The book reflects on human relationships nurtured in loving without fancy or waste. Many deep elements touched life's daily flow of processes, especially when the old patriarch is anchored in wisdom and grace. Dadu and Didima's stable assurance of dignity and impartial affection set the tone of harmony into the new generations.

Life was just as good, or way better without the gadgets and gimmicks of our overloaded modern life. The joys were tucked into simple moments of wondering and wandering, in loving and laughing, in making mistakes and discoveries.

Made in the USA
Middletown, DE
13 March 2022

62551613R00071